First Facts®

The
FIRST OLYMPICS
of
Ancient Greece

by Lisa M. Bolt Simons

Consultant:
Jonathan M. Hall
Phyllis Fay Horton Distinguished Service Professor
in the Humanities
The University of Chicago

CAPSTONE PRESS
a capstone imprint

First Facts are published by Capstone Press,
1710 Roe Crest Drive, North Mankato, Minnesota 56003
www.capstonepub.com

Library of Congress Cataloging-in-Publication Data
Simons, Lisa M. B., 1969–
The first Olympics of ancient Greece / Lisa M. Bolt Simons.
pages cm.—(Ancient Greece)
Includes bibliographical references and index.
ISBN 978-1-4914-0273-3 (library binding)
ISBN 978-1-4914-0278-8 (eBook PDF)
Summary: "Describes the events and ceremonies involved with the original Olympic games in ancient Greece."—Provided by publisher.
1. Olympic games (Ancient)—Juvenile literature. I. Title.
GV23.S52 2015
796.48—dc23   2013049474

Editorial Credits

Aaron Sautter, editor; Bobbie Nuytten, designer; Svetlana Zhurkin, media researcher; Jennifer Walker, production specialist

Photo Credits

Alamy: Chronicle, 9, North Wind Picture Archives, 19, The Art Gallery Collection, 15 (top); Bridgeman Art Library: Look and Learn/Private Collection/Race of the Four Horse Chariots, Salinas, Alberto (1932-2004), 11; Corbis: National Geographic Society, 13; National Geographic Creative: H.M. Herget, 5; Newscom: akg-images, 6, EPA/Michael Kappeler, 20, Universal Images Group/Leemage, 17; Shutterstock: Attsetski (wreath), 21, Brian Maudsley, cover (front), 15 (bottom), Ensuper (paper), back cover and throughout, Henner Damke, 18, ilolab (grunge background), cover, 1, Kamira, back cover (bottom right), 10, Maxim Kostenko (background), 2 and throughout, mexrix, 7 (back), Netfalls Remy Musser, cover (back), 1, Roberto Castillo (column), back cover and throughout, Tatiana Popova, 8; XNR Productions, 7 (map)

Printed in China by Nordica
0414/CA21400593
032014   008095NORDF14

TABLE OF CONTENTS

LET THE GAMES BEGIN!

Imagine you're in ancient Greece more than 2,700 years ago. Purple-robed judges, a trumpeter, and a **herald** enter the arena. Several horse-drawn **chariots** soon follow. The crowd roars as athletes' names are announced. It's time for the Olympic games!

FACT:
Greek athletes usually competed while naked to celebrate the human body and honor the gods.

Chariot races were a popular event in the ancient Olympics.

herald—an official at a competition who makes announcements to the crowd

chariot—a light two-wheeled cart pulled by horses

The first Olympics took place in 776 BC. The games were held in Olympia. Only male Greek **citizens** could compete in the games. The Olympics lasted for five days every four years during a full summer moon. The moonlight allowed events and celebrations to continue into the night.

Olympia was home to several temples to the gods.

citizen—a member of a country or state who has the right to live there

Ancient Greece, around 400 BC
• city-state (a city that is independent and is not part of a country)

Illyria

Macedonia

Epirus

Mt. Olympus ▲

Thessaly

Aegean Sea

Lesbos

Euboea

Delphi •

Thebes •

Attica

Corinth •

• Athens

Olympia •

• Argos

Peloponnesus

• Sparta

Rhodes

N
W   E
S

0   90 miles

0   90 kilometers

Crete

Mediterranean Sea

FACT:

No fighting or battles took place while the Olympics were held. The Greeks wanted athletes, trainers, and their families to be able to travel to the games in peace.

BEFORE THE GAMES

Before the opening **ceremony**, athletes, trainers, and judges took an **oath**. They promised to follow the rules and compete fairly. They also offered **sacrifices** of fruit and bronze items to the gods. Athletes prayed to the gods for victory.

ceremony—special actions, words, or music performed to mark an important event

oath—a serious, formal promise

sacrifice—something offered as a gift to a god

bronze shield from ancient Greece

FACT:

On the third morning of the Olympics, another ceremony was held at the Temple of Zeus. Priests sacrificed 100 oxen to honor the king of the gods.

Athletes honored Zeus at his temple in Olympia.

HORSE RACING EVENTS

Equestrian events had two kinds of races. Chariot races featured two- and four-horse chariots. Horses pulled the chariots for 12 laps around two poles in the hippodrome. These poles were about .25 mile (0.4 kilometer) apart. Regular horse races had six laps. The horse owners, not the riders, won the events.

ancient Greek vase with image of a chariot racer

equestrian—having to do with horses
hippodrome—a large oval arena used for horse and chariot races

A DANGEROUS, YET THRILLING SPORT

Chariot racing was a dangerous sport. Chariot drivers often took risks. Sometimes they moved to the inside during tight turns. The move sometimes helped them get a lead. But it often resulted in crashes and serious injuries.

RUNNING EVENTS

The stadion was a 192-meter (630-foot) race. It was the first and only event of the original Olympics in 776 BC. Eventually more races were added. These included races of 200 meters (656 feet), 400 meters (1,312 feet), and 4,800 meters (15,748 feet). Racers ran barefoot on a track made of sand. Up to 20 athletes could run side by side.

FACT:

One Olympic race featured athletes wearing armor and a helmet. They ran 400 meters (1,312 feet) while carrying a shield.

TRACK AND FIELD

The pentathlon was similar to modern track-and-field events. It included a running race, long jumping, wrestling, **discus** throwing, and **javelin** throwing. The race was a sprint of almost 200 meters (656 feet). Athletes held weights in their hands for the long jump event. Wrestlers won by making an opponent fall three times. In discus and javelin events, athletes threw each object five times. The athlete with the longest throw won.

discus—a large heavy disk that is thrown for distance in a competition

javelin—a light spear that is thrown for distance in a competition

discus-throwing competition in ancient Greece

THREE EVENTS OR FIVE?

Pentathlon contestants sometimes competed in only three events. If an athlete won the discus, javelin, and long jump events, he was declared the pentathlon winner. If nobody won all three, athletes then competed in running and wrestling events.

BOXING AND WRESTLING

There were few rules in wrestling and boxing events. There was no ring and no time limit. A wrestler lost if he fell to his knees three times. Boxers won with a **knockout** or if an opponent raised his right hand to signal defeat. The pankration event was a mix of boxing, wrestling, and **martial arts**.

knockout—a victory when a fighter's opponent is unable to get up after being knocked to the ground
martial arts—styles of self-defense and fighting

FACT:

During pankration matches, athletes could do almost anything to win. They could slap, punch, and kick their opponents. An athlete won when his opponent gave up by tapping him on the shoulder or back.

AWARD CEREMONIES

Each event had two award ceremonies. Judges first gave palm branches to the event winners. Red ribbons were also tied to winners' heads and hands. On the last day of the games, the winners for all the events were announced. Olive tree wreaths were then placed on their heads.

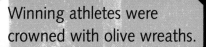

Winning athletes were crowned with olive wreaths.

FACT:

Leonidas of Rhodes was the most successful athlete of the ancient Olympics. He won all his events in four straight Olympic games for a total of 12 olive wreaths.

ANCIENT VS. MODERN OLYMPICS

Today's Olympics have changed from the ancient games. The modern games are held in different cities around the world every two years. They include various winter and summer events. Ancient Greek athletes competed as individuals. Today's athletes often compete in teams from all over the world. The modern Olympics have changed over time, but the spirit of the ancient games lives on.

the 2012 Summer Olympics in London, England

The Athletes Who Became Legends

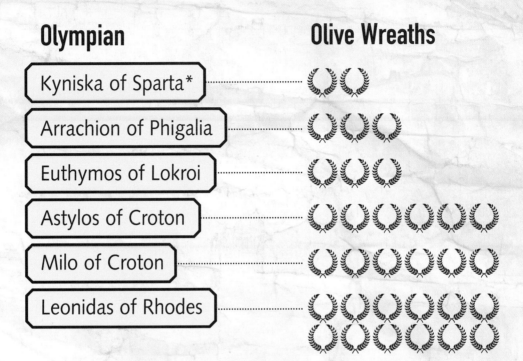

Olympian	Olive Wreaths
Kyniska of Sparta*	🏆🏆
Arrachion of Phigalia	🏆🏆🏆
Euthymos of Lokroi	🏆🏆🏆
Astylos of Croton	🏆🏆🏆🏆🏆🏆
Milo of Croton	🏆🏆🏆🏆🏆🏆
Leonidas of Rhodes	🏆🏆🏆🏆🏆🏆🏆🏆🏆🏆🏆🏆

*the first woman to win; she was a horse owner

FACT:

In his last two Olympics, Astylos competed for Syracuse instead of his home city of Croton. This angered the people in Croton. They tore down the statue of Astylos and made his house into a prison.

Glossary

ceremony (SAYR-uh-moh-nee)—special actions, words, or music performed to mark an important event

chariot (CHAYR-ee-uht)—a light, two-wheeled cart pulled by horses

citizen (SI-tuh-zuhn)—a member of a country or state who has the right to live there

city-state (SI-tee-STAYT)—a city that is independent and is not part of a country

discus (DISS-kuhss)—a large heavy disk that is thrown for distance in a track-and-field event

equestrian (i-KWES-tree-uhn)—having to do with horses

herald (HAIR-ahld)—an official at a competition who makes announcements to the crowd

hippodrome (HIP-uh-drohm)—a large oval arena used for horse and chariot races

javelin (JAV-uh-luhn)—a light spear that is thrown for distance in a track-and-field event

knockout (NOK-out)—a victory when a fighter's opponent is unable to get up after being knocked to the ground

martial arts (MAR-shuhl ARTS)—styles of self-defense and fighting

oath (OHTH)—a serious, formal promise

sacrifice (SAK-ruh-fisse)—something offered as a gift to a god

Read More

Butterfield, Moira. *The Olympics: History*. The Olympics. Mankato, Minn.: Sea-to-Sea Publications, 2012.

Mason, Paul. *Sports Heroes of Ancient Greece*. Crabtree Connections. New York: Crabtree Pub. Co., 2011.

Newman, Sandra. *Ancient Greece*. A True Book. New York: Children's Press, 2010.

Internet Sites

FactHound offers a safe, fun way to find Internet sites related to this book. All of the sites on FactHound have been researched by our staff.

Here's all you do:

Visit *www.facthound.com*

Type in this code: 9781491402733

Super-cool stuff!

Check out projects, games and lots more at
www.capstonekids.com

Critical Thinking Using the Common Core

1. Why do you think ancient Greek athletes and trainers offered sacrifices to the gods before the Olympic games began? (Integration of Knowledge and Ideas)

2. Name the five events of the pentathlon and explain two ways an athlete could become the overall pentathlon winner. (Key Ideas and Details)

Index